An A-Maze-ing Colorful Journey

Undersea Adventure Mazes

Roger Moreau

Sterling Publishing Co., Inc.
New York

This book is dedicated to
Alex, Andrew, Brian, Austin,
Krista, Max, Lauren, David, and ?

4   6   8   10   9   7   5

Published by Sterling Publishing Co., Inc.

387 Park Avenue South, New York, NY 10016

© 2004 by Roger Moreau

Distributed in Canada by Sterling Publishing

c/o Canadian Manda Group,165 Dufferin Street, Toronto,

Ontario, Canada M6K 3H6

Distributed in the United Kingdom by GMC Distribution Services,

Castle Place, 166 High Street, Lewes, East Sussex, England BN7 1XU

Distributed in Australia by Capricorn Link (Australia) Pty. Ltd.

P.O. Box 704, Windsor, NSW 2756, Australia

Printed in China

1-4027-0908-0

Contents

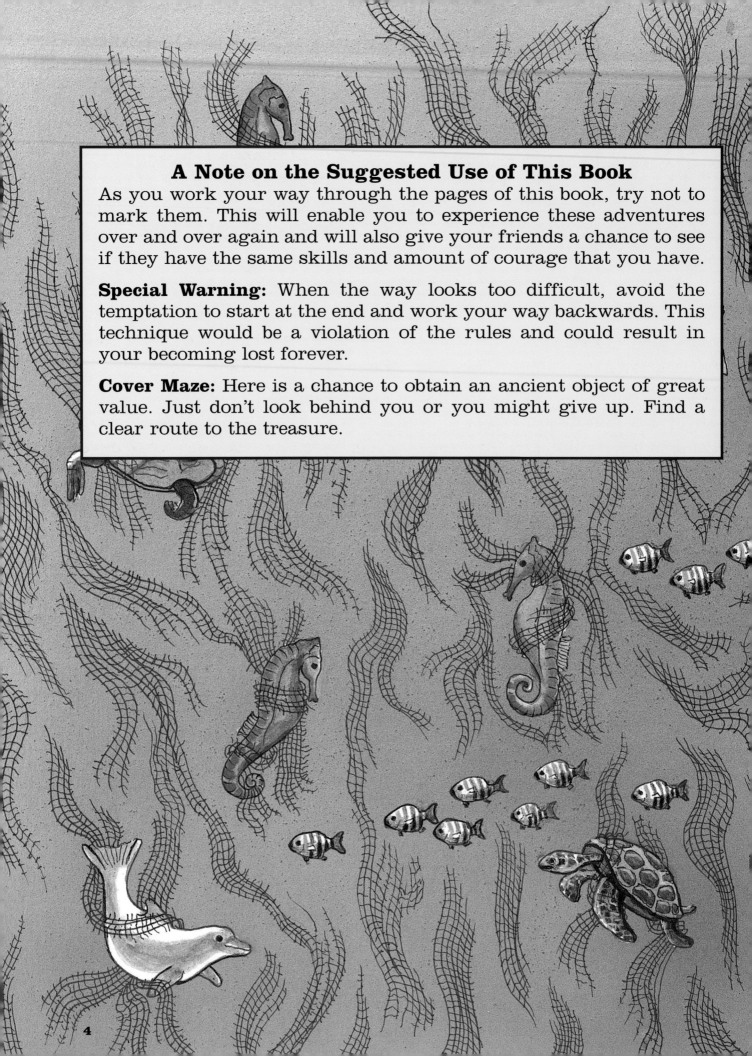

A Note on the Suggested Use of This Book

As you work your way through the pages of this book, try not to mark them. This will enable you to experience these adventures over and over again and will also give your friends a chance to see if they have the same skills and amount of courage that you have.

Special Warning: When the way looks too difficult, avoid the temptation to start at the end and work your way backwards. This technique would be a violation of the rules and could result in your becoming lost forever.

Cover Maze: Here is a chance to obtain an ancient object of great value. Just don't look behind you or you might give up. Find a clear route to the treasure.

Introduction

There exists beneath the surface of the ocean a completely different world from the one we live in. Great areas of water cover 70.8 percent of the earth's surface, an area so vast that even though there has been a great deal of exploration, only about 10 percent of what lies beneath the surface is known to man. To go into that world for any length of time requires special equipment not only to stay alive, but also to be able to see. And then you can see only to the depths that the sunlight can reach. After that, the sunlight fades and the depths become pitch-black. To explore these depths, you would have to bring your own light.

Life is abundant in the oceans. Its creatures, for the most part, fear humans and quickly swim away or hide. But there are some that have no fear, that will aggressively attack and eat a human if they get a chance. Others have defensive abilities to camouflage themselves (for example, by changing colors) or inflict pain (for example, by injecting poison) to protect themselves. Underwater explorers must always be cautious and on guard for the unexpected.

Over the years of human endeavor upon the sea, ships, treasures, and objects of all kinds have ended up on the ocean floor. Those near the surface can be easily explored and salvaged, but in the deeper depths this becomes more difficult, if not impossible. It is often a major challenge just to locate a ship or treasure. But, thanks to modern technology and the tenacity of explorers, many great discoveries are being made not only at finding man-made objects, but also with regard to undersea geology.

In the following adventures, you will have a chance to go under the sea to explore, learn, and discover. As with any adventure, it is always helpful to know what to expect so that you can prepare for what you might encounter. Here is a preview.

Get Ready for the Adventure Ahead

It would be a good idea to start out with a routine practice dive. Once you've completed that, get ready for some really important dives.

There is no question that a great deal of treasure has been lost in the depths of the ocean. Wouldn't it be great to continue your adventure by finding and retrieving a large and valuable treasure? You'll get that chance.

The next phase of your experience will be to find and study some of the most interesting and dangerous life in the ocean. Giant squid have never been seen alive, although they are known to exist. The great white shark is always a danger. Did you know that a coelacanth, a fish thought to be extinct for 50 million years, was caught off the coast of South Africa in 1938? Several more have been seen alive since and now you'll get a chance to see one. Whales are huge animals that require air to breathe. They will be near the surface, so you'll get a chance to examine several different types of whales without having to dive deep.

Careless fishermen sometimes harm life in the sea when they get entangled in their fishing equipment. Their only chance of help would be from a caring human. Take the opportunity to rescue them if you come across any.

A lot of ships have been sunk and are historical relics waiting to be explored. You will have the chance to find and study some of these ships. You'll get an opportunity to do other special things regarding this unique experience. Enjoy this phase of your exploration.

Finally, dive to the deepest depth . . . if you dare. 35,800 feet is a long way down, almost seven miles. This will be tough. The sea life will be unique. Who knows what you might discover—possibly a life form that has never been seen before!

Good luck. Don't get discouraged if your way becomes tough or appears dangerous, and enjoy your adventure. Be safe.

The Eel

Find a clear route down to study this unfriendly looking eel.

The Sacrificial Aztec Blade

This treasure is yours for the taking if you find a clear route around the coral and sea life.

The Paper Scroll

Find a clear route and pick up this paper scroll. It could be important.

A Treasure Map

That scroll is a treasure map. Plot your way around the coral reefs and islands to the X that marks the spot.

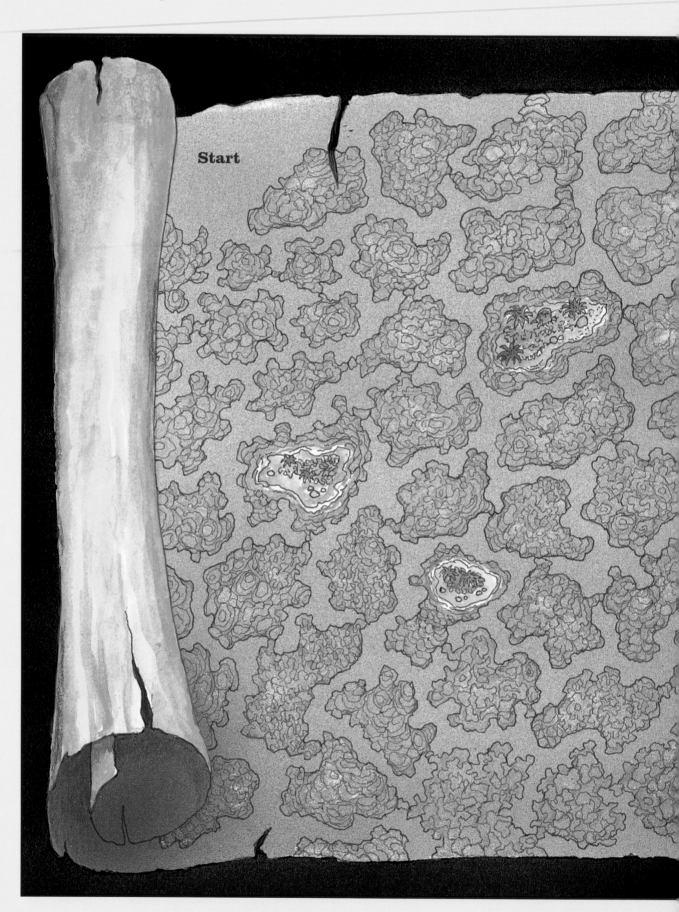

Start

End

The Treasure

The treasure is yours if you can survive finding a clear route to it.

Start

End

Ancient Amphora Bottles

Take the basket down and pick up these ancient amphora bottles. Find a clear route.

The Roman Statue

Find a clear route to pick up this Roman statue.

The Giant Squid

Here is a special chance to study the rare and elusive giant squid. Find a clear route and get right up close . . . if you dare.

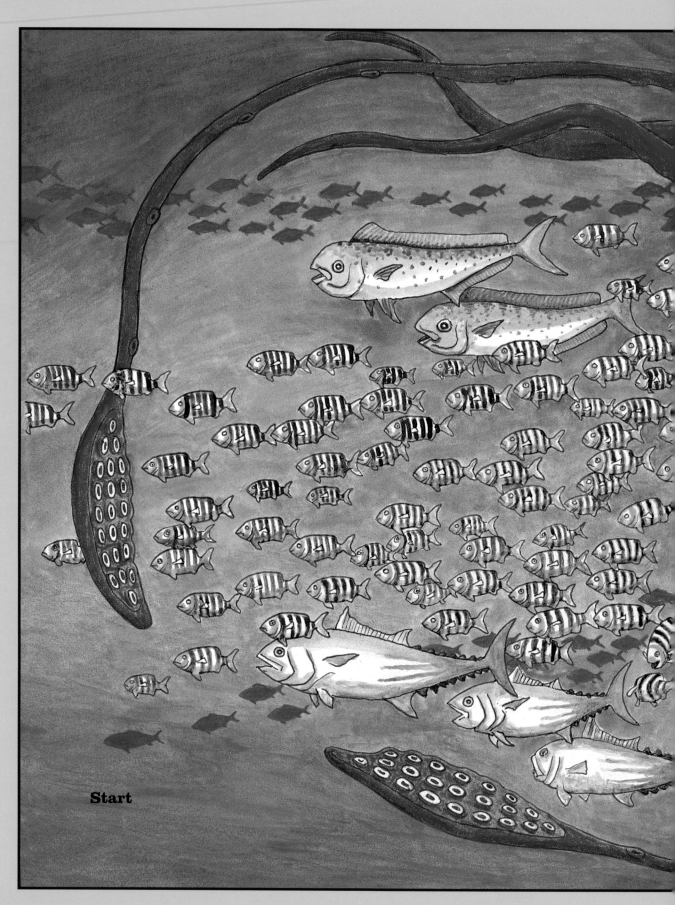

Start

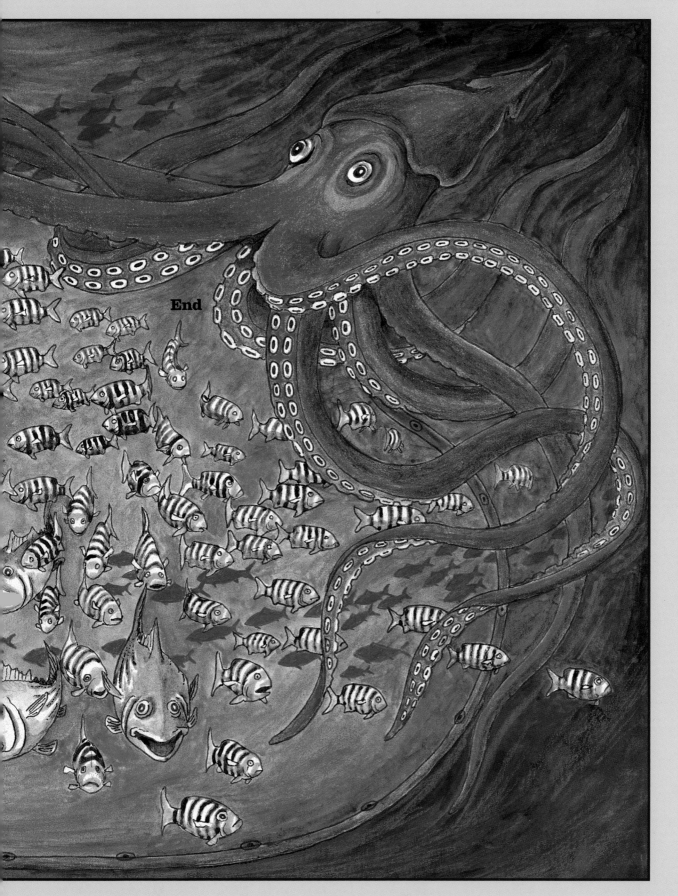

End

The Great White Shark

It took courage to study the squid. Now study the great white shark. Find a clear route.

Start

End

A Coelacanth . . . Wow!

Study this rare prehistoric fish up close. Find a clear route.

Start

End

Six Whales

Here are six different kinds of whales. Study each one by finding a route to the face of each whale. Start anywhere above the water. Do not backtrack or cross over your route, and find your way back to the surface.

Start

End

Reach the North Pole

Avoid the polar bears. Dive under the ice and find a clear route to the North Pole.

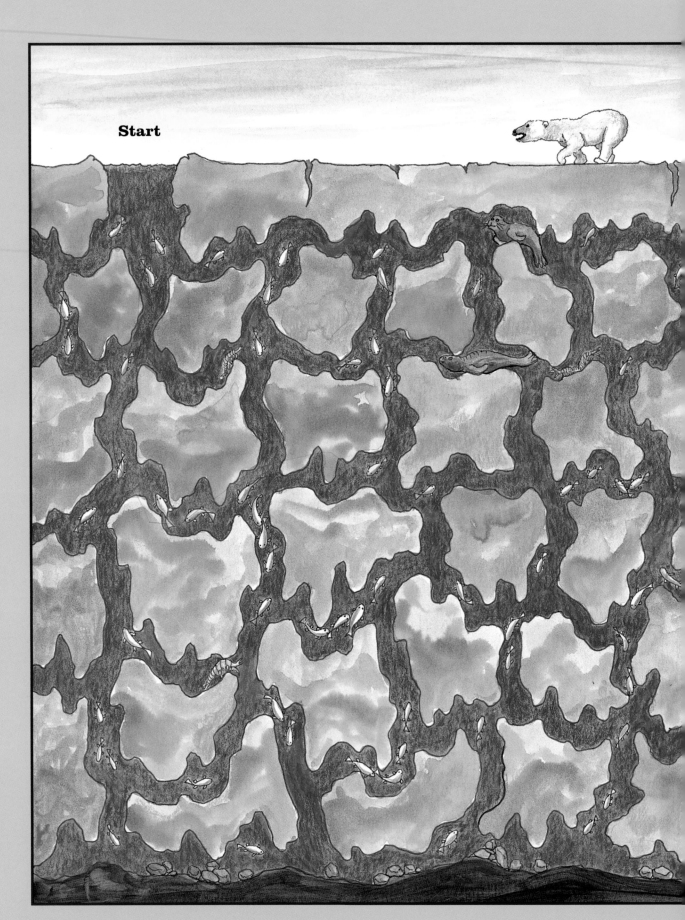

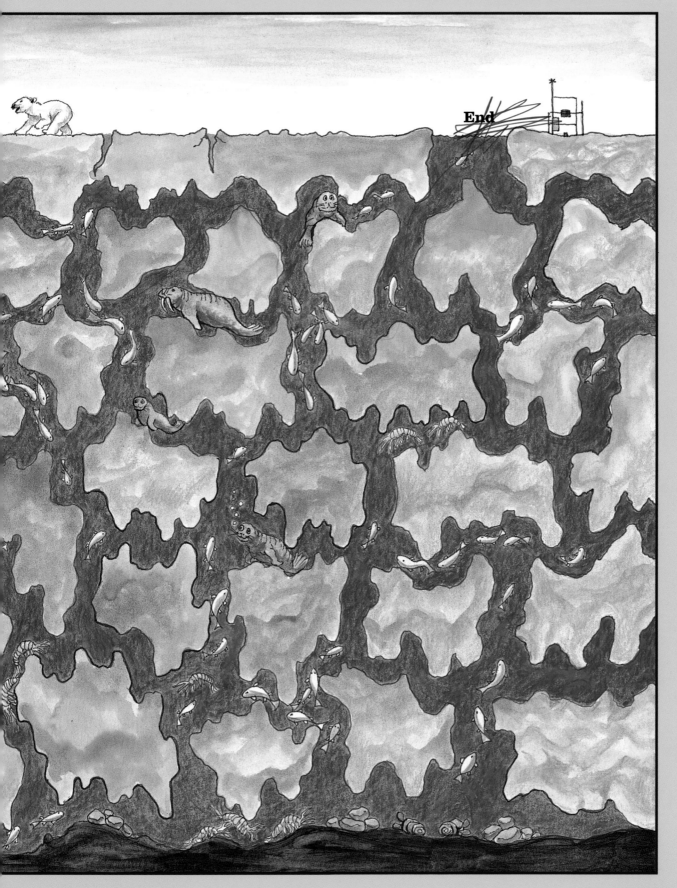

End

Terrible Gill Nets

Free each sea creature by finding a route to each. Do not backtrack or cross over your route. Continue on to the next maze.

Start

Continue the Rescue

Continue downward and save each sea creature.

End

Save the Sea Lion

That poor sea lion will need air. Dive down and free him from the netting. Find a clear route. Hurry!

End

Moby Dick

Moby Dick, the great white whale, has had that spear in him too long. Find a clear route and pull it out.

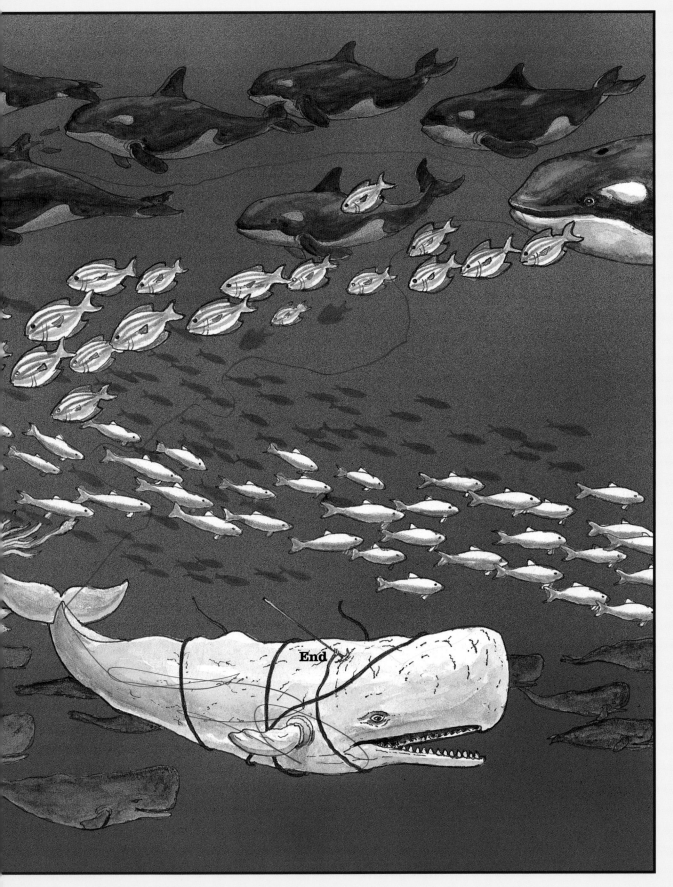

End

The Battleship *Arizona*

Sunk in Pearl Harbor at the start of World War II, the battleship *Arizona* is a resting place for the sailors who died on her. Find a clear route and place a wreath inside her hull.

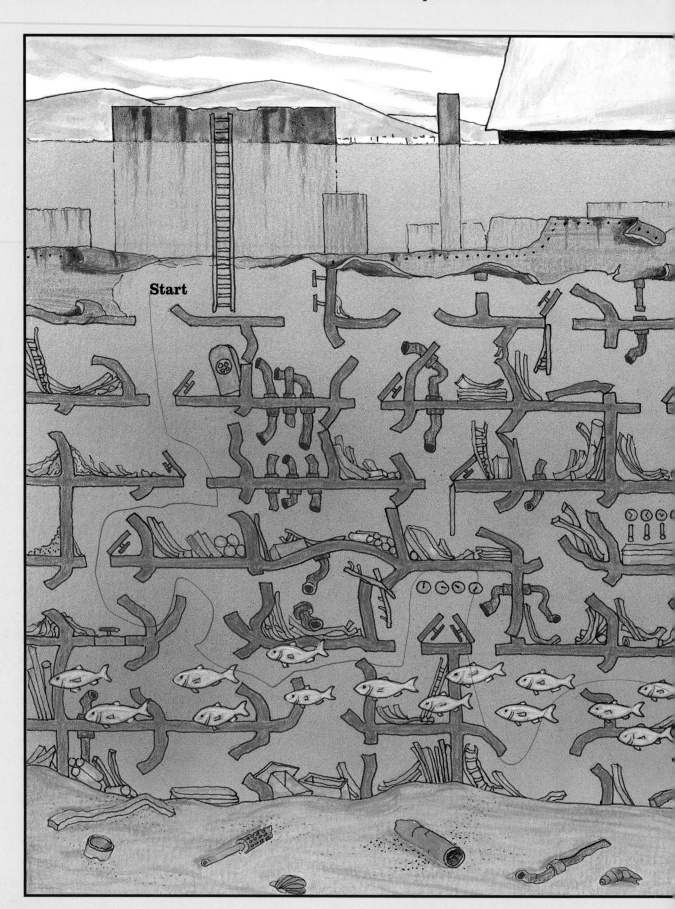

Start

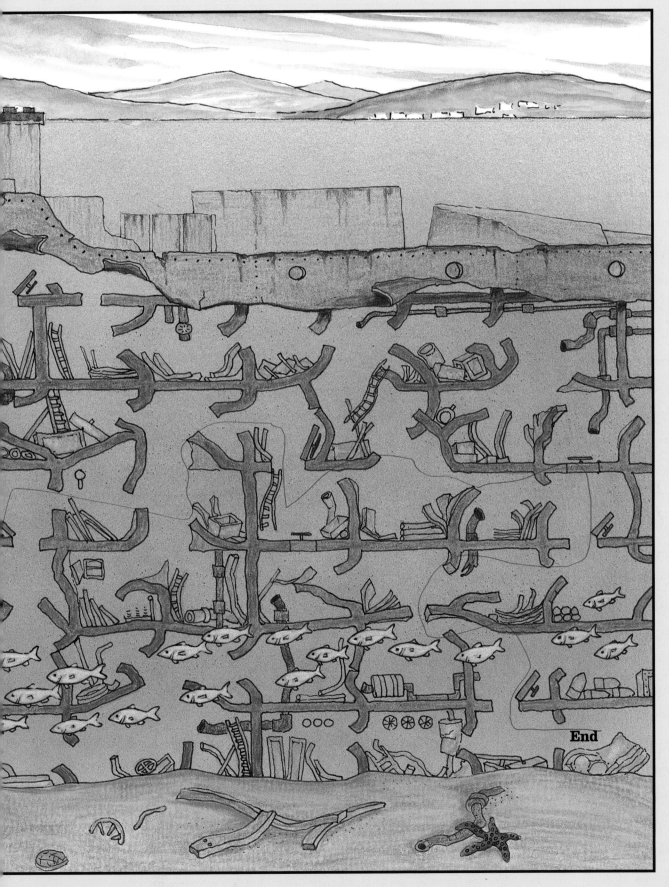

End

The Battle of Midway

During World War II, four enemy carriers were sunk in the battle of Midway. Start at the bottom of the grid. Find a continual path to each carrier through the openings in the grid.

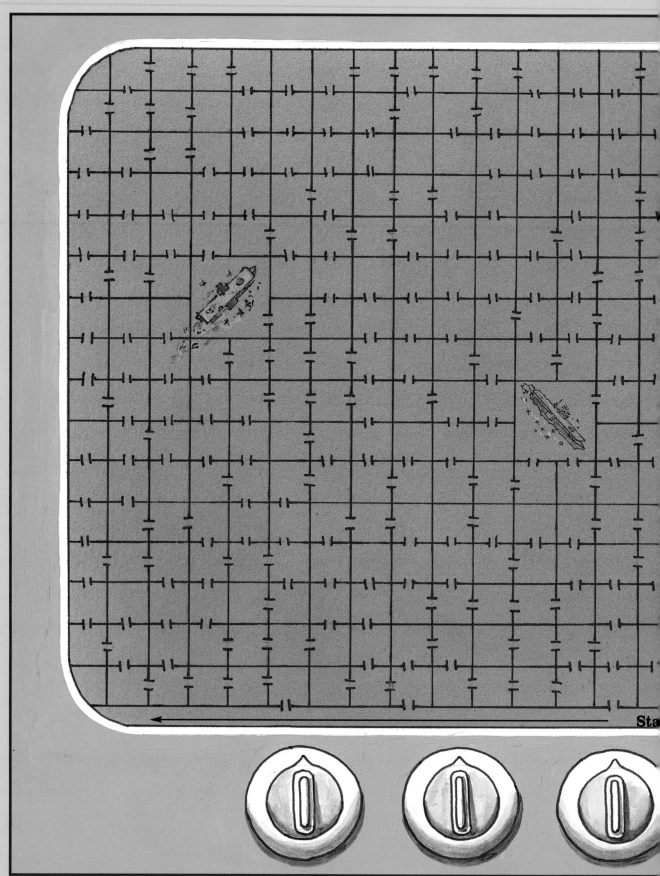

Sta

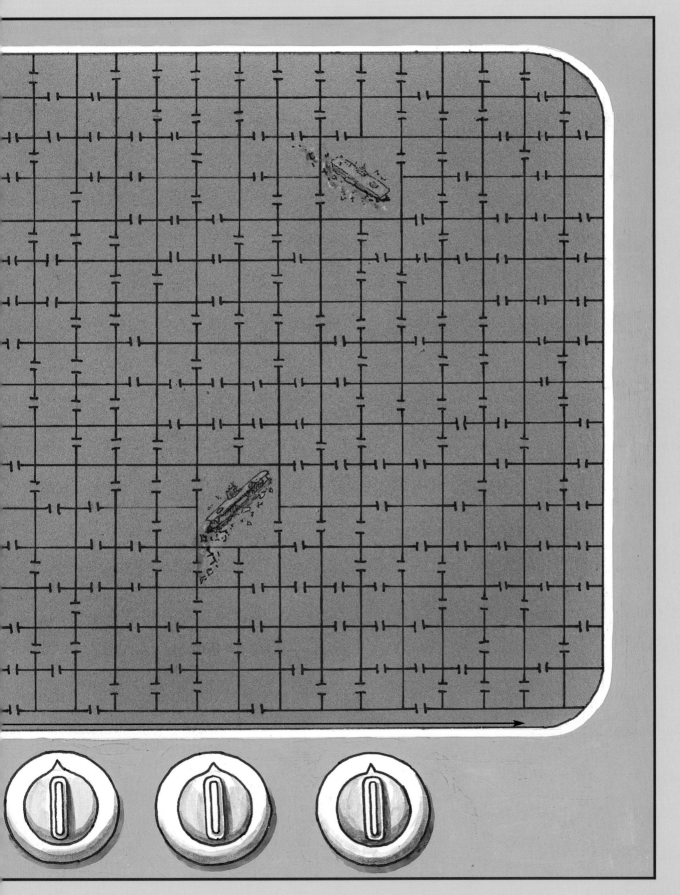

The Carrier *Akagi*

Explore the deck of the sunken carrier *Akagi*. Find a clear route to the front of the carrier and continue exploring its deck.

The *Wahoo*

What happened to the United States submarine *Wahoo* that disappeared during World War II? Is that the *Wahoo*? Find a clear route to the sub and see.

Start

End

Iron Bottom Sound

This is a graveyard of sunken ships. Notice that there is a *live* bomb on the bottom. Find a clear route to the bomb and disarm it.

End

Raise the *Titanic*

Hoses have been hooked up to flotation bags to raise the *Titanic*, but one has come loose. Find the correct hose and follow it down to hook it back up.

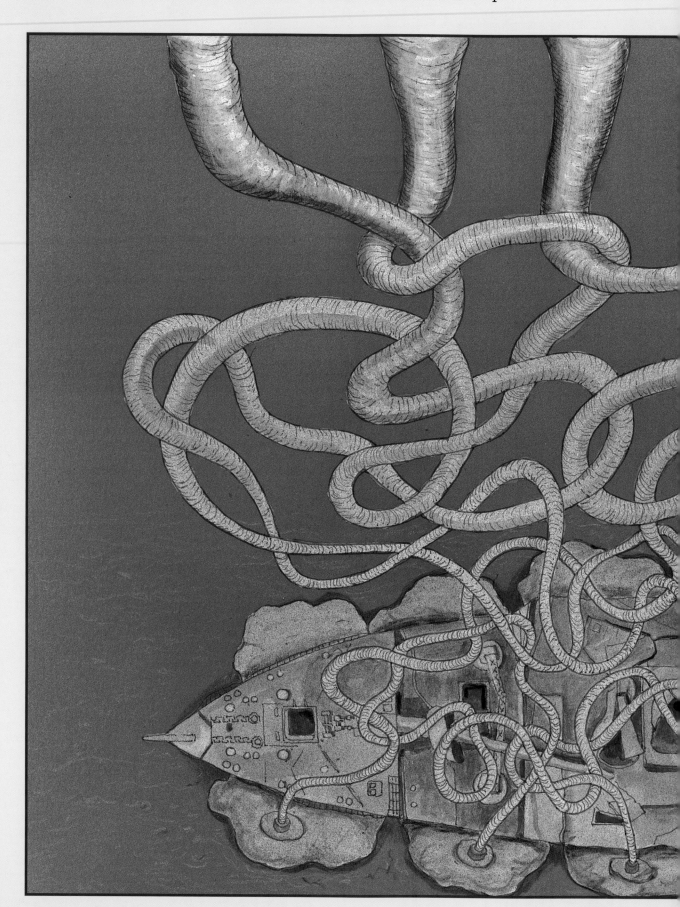

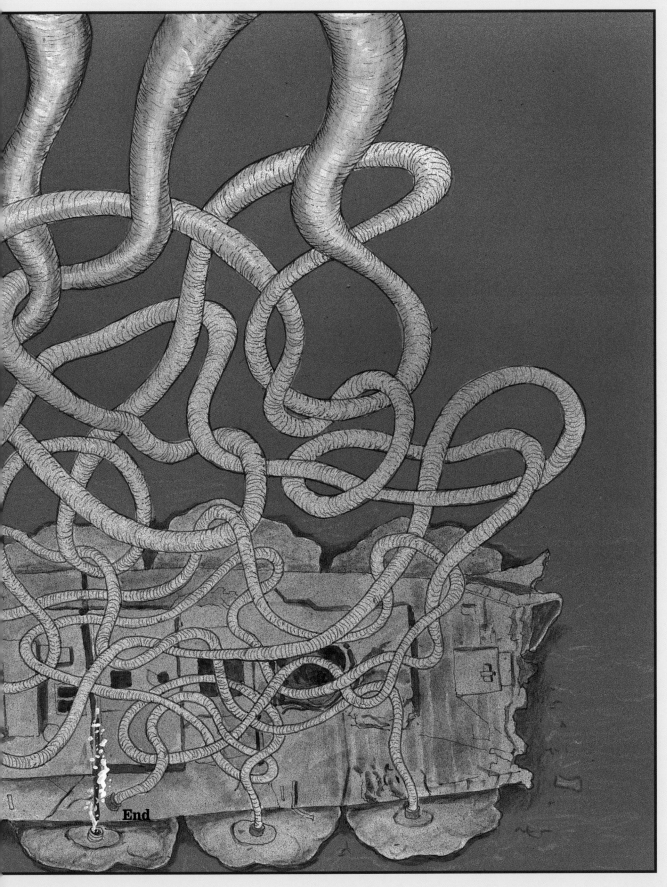

End

The Transatlantic Cable

The cable is broken in four places. Find a clear route down and fix each of the breaks.

Start

End

The Mid-Atlantic Rift

This crack in the deep Atlantic, known as the Mid-Atlantic Rift, is giving off heat and steam. Find a clear route to explore the crack.

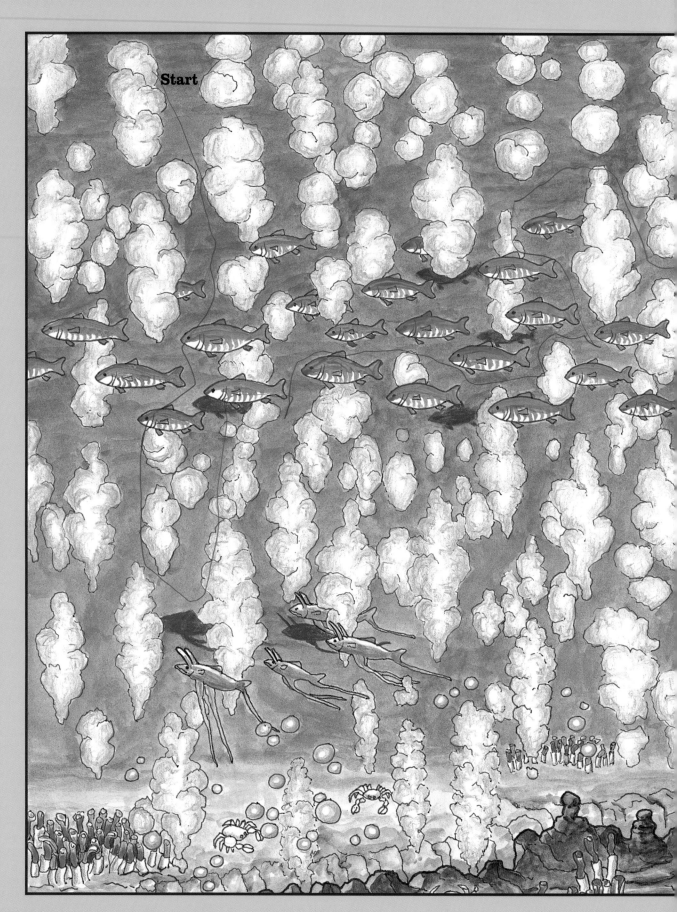

Start

46

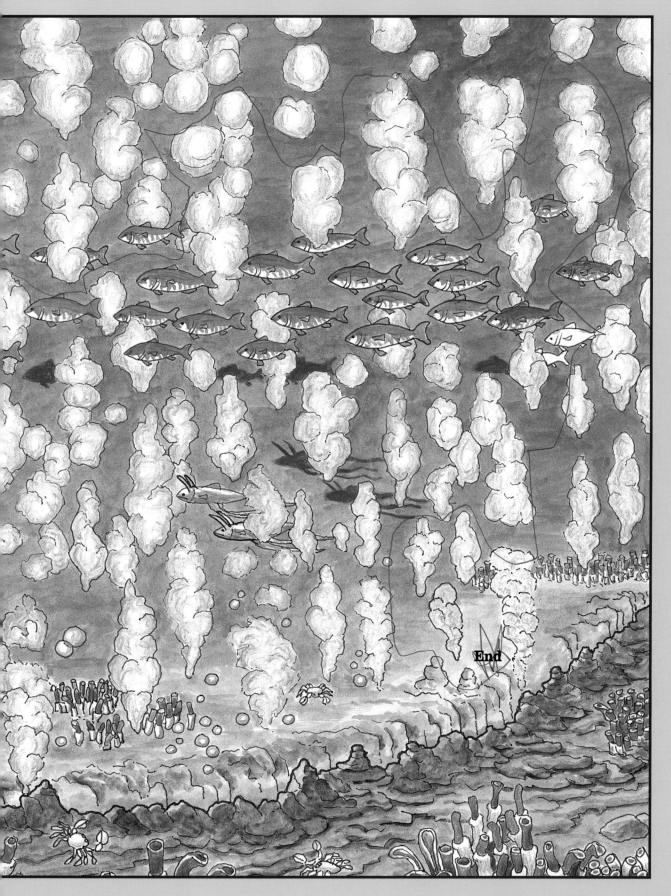

End

Hold Your Breath

Hold your breath and dive 35,800 feet down to the bottom of the Mariana Trench, the deepest spot in the ocean. Start anywhere at the top and find a clear route to the bottom of the page and continue on to the next maze.

The Mariana Trench

Continue down . . . don't give up. If you make it, it will be a record dive.

End

Mermaids?

After that deep dive, could your eyes be deceiving you? Are those mermaids? Find a clear route and find out.

Start

End

Congratulations!

You have just completed and survived this exciting and dangerous adventure that has taken you under the sea, where you have had a chance to view the many wonders, hidden secrets, and interesting life that exist there. It has not been easy. It has required courage. You've had to face the unknown and unpredictable nature of the sea creatures that you came in contact with. But you didn't give up and now know that perseverance is a quality that can bring great rewards. Rewards that you have earned as a product of completing this experience.

If you had any problems along the way, refer to the solutions to the mazes on the following pages.

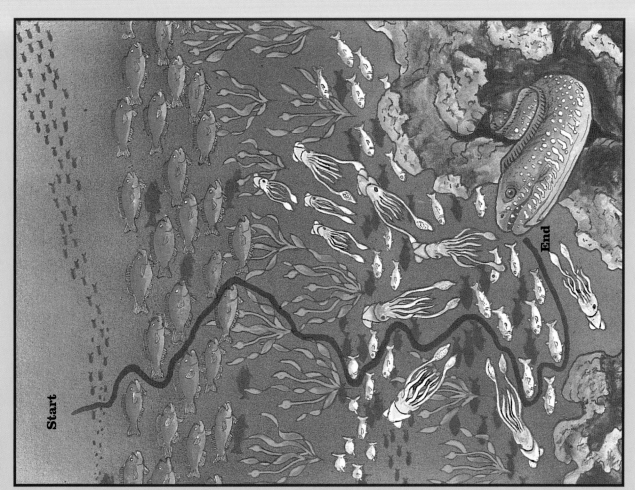

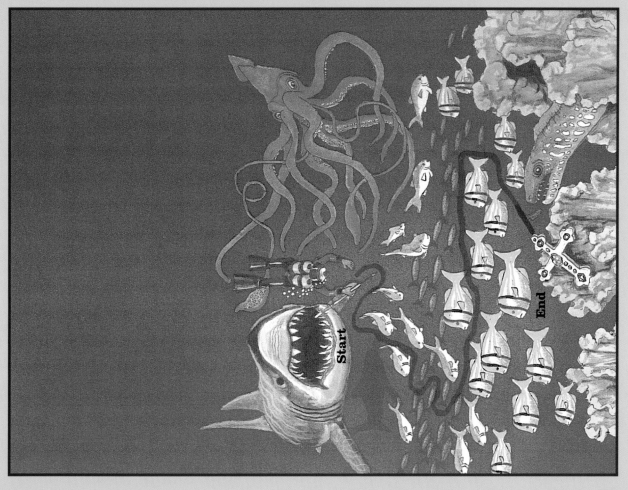

The Sacrificial Aztec Blade

Start

End

The Paper Scroll

Start

End

A Treasure Map

Start

End

The Treasure

Start

End

Ancient Amphora Bottles

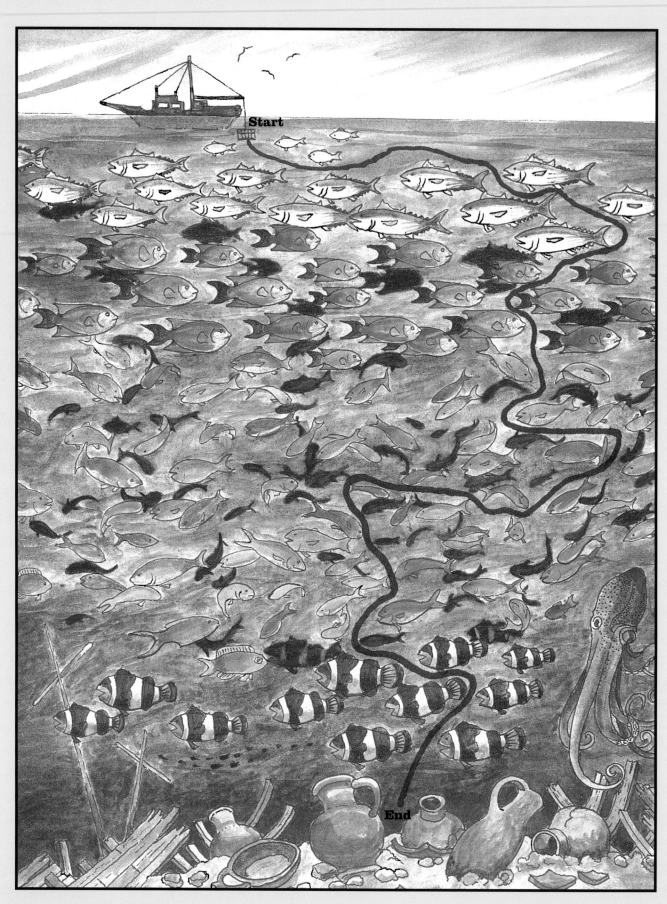

Start

End

The Roman Statue

Start

End

The Giant Squid

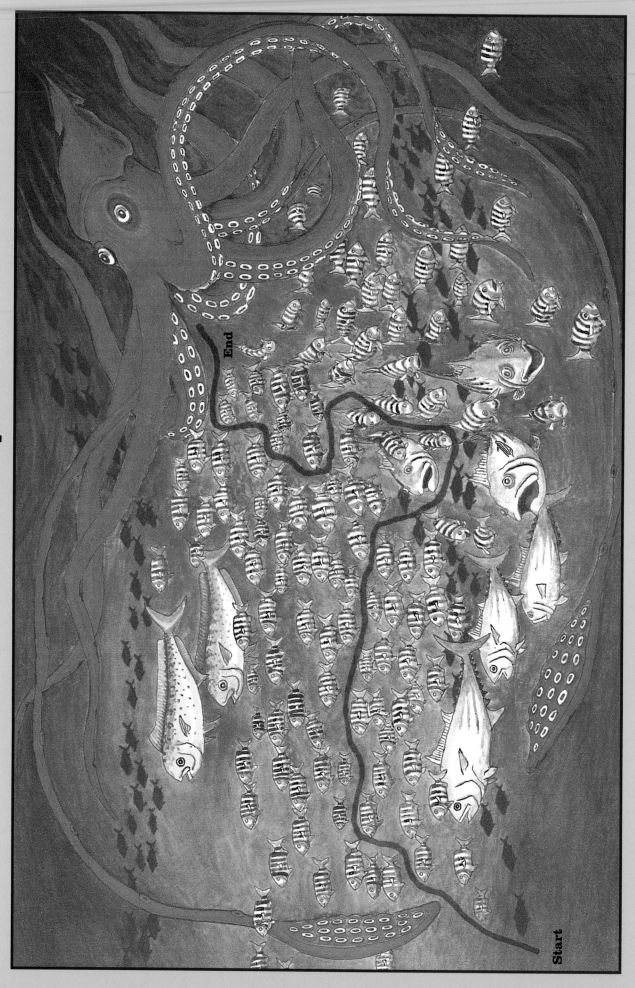

Start

End

The Great White Shark

Start

End

A Coelacanth . . . Wow!

Start

End

Six Whales

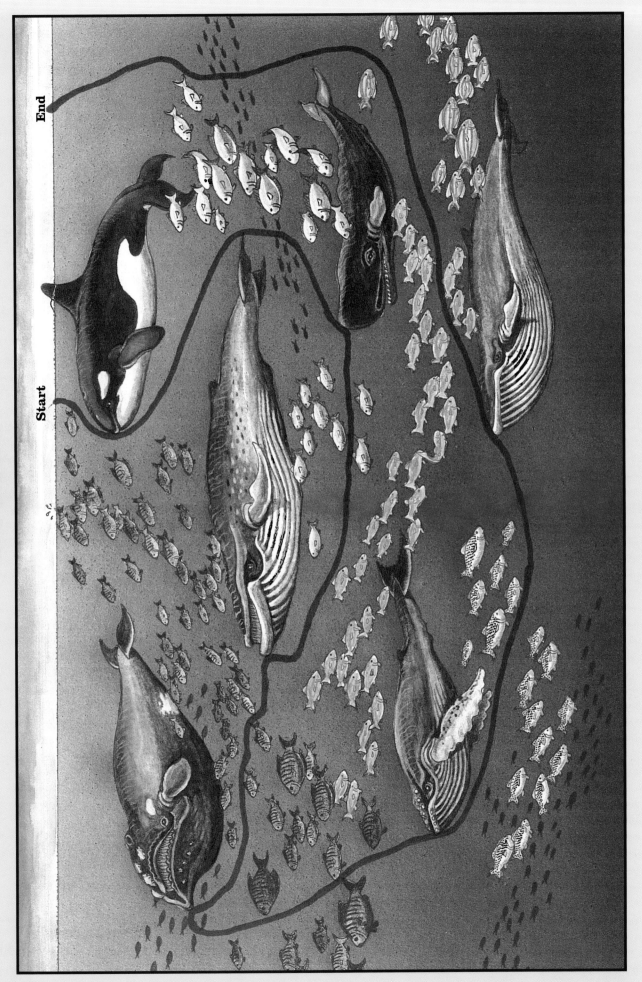

Start

End

Reach the North Pole

End

Terrible Gill Nets

Start

Continue the Rescue

End

Save the Sea Lion

Start

End

Moby Dick

Start

End

The Battleship *Arizona*

Start

End

The Battle of Midway

The Carrier *Akagi*

Start

End

The *Wahoo*

Start

End

Iron Bottom Sound

Start

End

Raise the _Titanic_

End

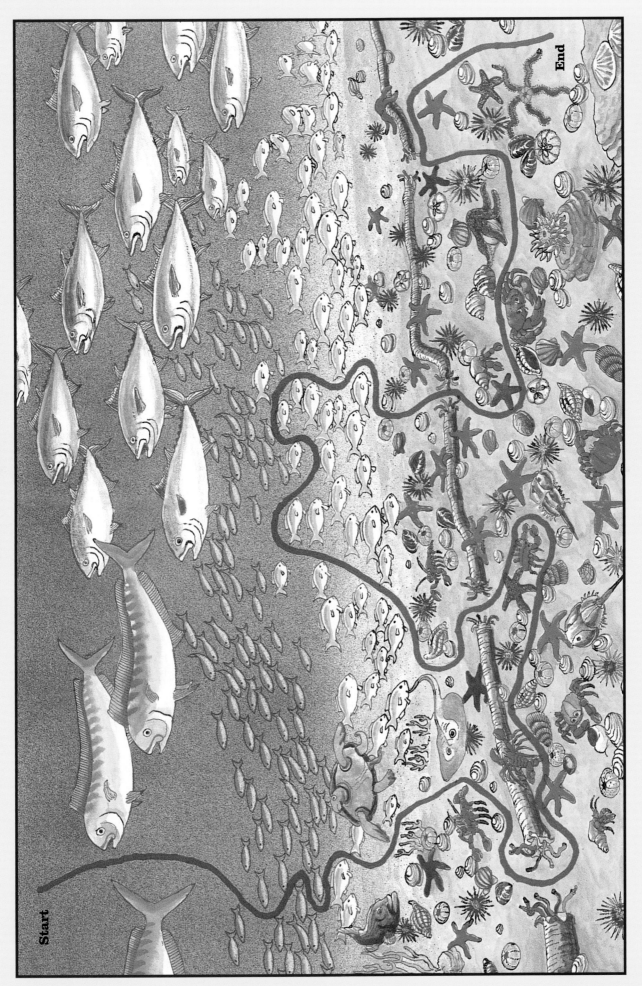

The Transatlantic Cable

Start

End

The Mid-Atlantic Rift

Start

End

Hold Your Breath

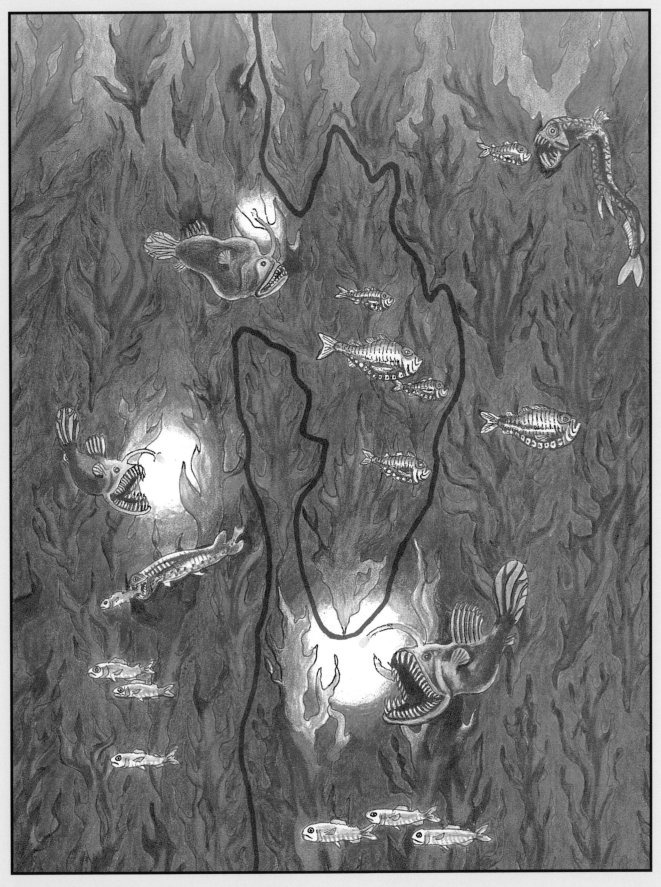

The Mariana Trench

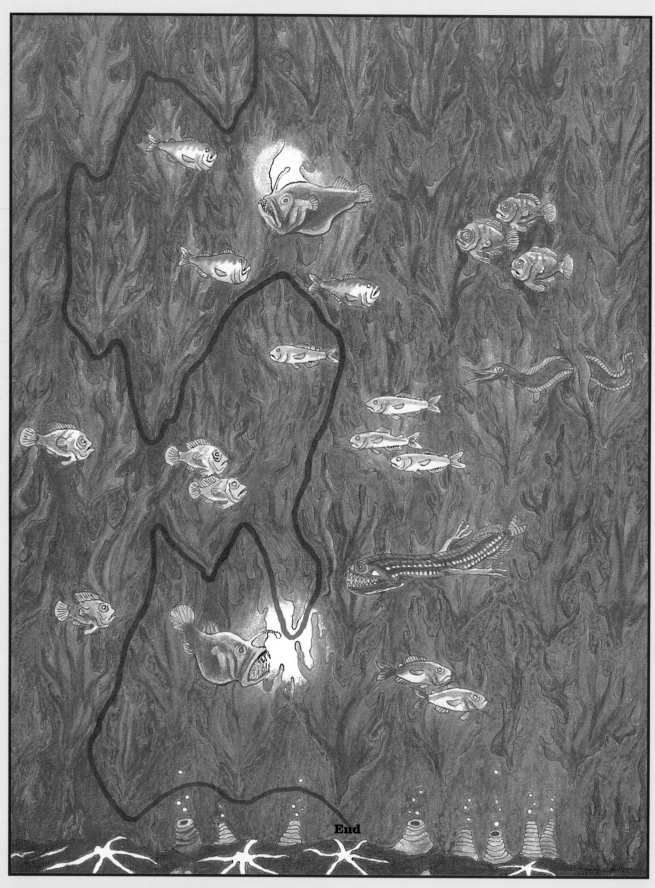

End

Mermaids?

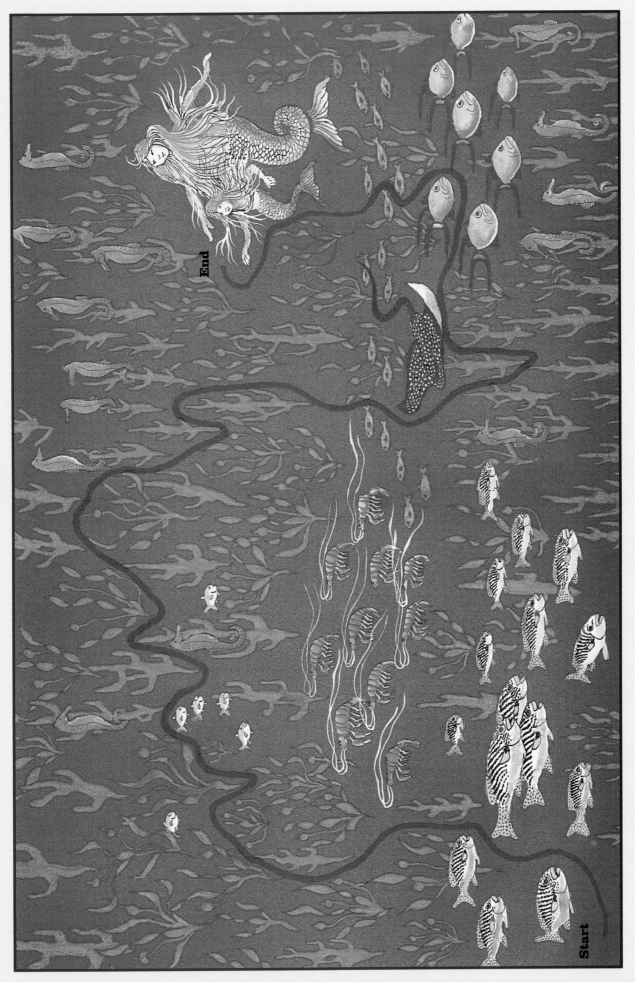

End

Start

Index

Page numbers in **bold** refer to answer mazes.